To: 3/27/05

Julie McGuire

From:

Leatha McGuire

May the God of hope fill
you with all joy.

Romans 15:13

Promises of Joy from the New International Version
Copyright ©2004 by The Zondervan Corporation
ISBN 0-310-80775-1

All Scripture quotations, unless otherwise noted, are taken from the *Holy Bible: New International Version, (North American Edition)*®. Copyright ©1973, 1978, 1984, by International Bible Society. Used by permission of Zondervan. All rights reserved.

The "NIV" and "New International Version" trademarks are registered in the United States Patent and Trademark Office by International Bible Society.

All rights reserved. No part of this publication may be reproduced, stored in a retrieval system, or transmitted in any form or by any means—electronic, mechanical, photocopy, recording, or any other—except for brief quotations in printed reviews, without the prior permission of the publisher.

Requests for information should be addressed to:
 Inspirio, The gift group of Zondervan
 Grand Rapids, Michigan 49530
 http://www.inspiriogifts.com

Project Manager and Compilation: Molly C. Detweiler
Design: Mark Veldheer
Cover Photo: ©DigitalVision/PictureQuest

Printed in China
04 05 06/HK/4 3 2 1

promises of Joy

from the
New International Version

Promises of Joy *in* Difficult Times

The joy of the LORD is your strength.

NEHEMIAH 8:10

God will keep you strong to the end, so that you will be blameless on the day of our Lord Jesus Christ.

1 Corinthians 1:8

The LORD gives strength to his people;
    the LORD blesses his people with peace.

Psalm 29:11

*The LORD is my strength and my shield;
    my heart trusts in him, and I am helped.
My heart leaps for joy
    and I will give thanks to him in song.
The LORD is the strength of his people,
    a fortress of salvation for his anointed one.*

Psalm 28:7–8

The God of all grace, who called you to his eternal glory in Christ, after you have suffered a little while, will himself restore you and make you strong, firm and steadfast.

1 Peter 5:10

*It is God who arms me with strength
and makes my way perfect.
He makes my feet like the feet of a deer;
he enables me to stand on the heights.*

Psalm 18:32–33

May our Lord Jesus Christ himself and God our Father, who loved us and by his grace gave us eternal encouragement and good hope, encourage your hearts and strengthen you in every good deed and word.

2 Thessalonians 2:16–17

The Spirit of the Sovereign LORD is on me,
because the LORD has anointed me
to preach good news to the poor.
He has sent me to bind up
the brokenhearted,...
to comfort all who mourn,
and provide for those who
grieve in Zion—
to bestow on them a crown of beauty
instead of ashes,
the oil of gladness
instead of mourning,
and a garment of praise
instead of a spirit of despair.

ISAIAH 61:1–3

Let all who take refuge in you be glad;
let them ever sing for joy.
Spread your protection over them,
that those who love your name may rejoice in you.
For surely, O LORD, you bless the righteous;
you surround them with your favor as with a shield.

Psalm 5:11–12

Are not two sparrows sold for a penny? Yet not one of them will fall to the ground apart from the will of your Father. And even the very hairs of your head are all numbered. So don't be afraid; you are worth more than many sparrows.

Matthew 10:29–31

Show me your ways, O LORD,
*   teach me your paths;*
guide me in your truth and teach me,
*   for you are God my Savior,*
*   and my hope is in you all day long.*
Remember, O LORD, your great
*   mercy and love,*
*   for they are from of old.*

Psalm 25:4–6

When anxiety was great
   within me,
   your consolation brought
      joy to my soul, O LORD.

Psalm 94:19

Jesus said, "I tell you the truth, you will weep and mourn while the world rejoices. You will grieve, but your grief will turn to joy.... Now is your time of grief, but I will see you again and you will rejoice, and no one will take away your joy."

John 16:20, 22

The Lord is faithful, and he will strengthen and protect you from the evil one.

2 Thessalonians 3:3

I can do everything through Christ who gives me strength.

Philippians 4:13

You answer us with awesome deeds
of righteousness,
O God our Savior,
the hope of all the ends of the earth
and of the farthest seas.

Psalm 65:5

I pray that out of God's glorious riches he may strengthen you with power through his Spirit in your inner being, so that Christ may dwell in your hearts through faith.

Ephesians 3:16–17

My soul is weary with sorrow;
strengthen me according
to your word, O LORD.

Psalm 119:28

Find rest, O my soul, in God alone;
my hope comes from him.
He alone is my rock and my salvation;
he is my fortress, I will not be shaken.

Psalm 62:5–6

The ransomed of the LORD will return.
They will enter Zion with singing;
everlasting joy will crown their heads.
Gladness and joy will overtake them,
and sorrow and sighing will flee away.

Isaiah 35:10

The eyes of the LORD are on
those who fear him,
on those whose hope
is in his unfailing love....
We wait in hope for the LORD;
he is our help and our shield.
In him our hearts rejoice,
for we trust in his holy name.
May your unfailing love rest
upon us, O LORD,
even as we put our hope in you.

PSALM 33:18, 20–22

May God strengthen your hearts so that you will be blameless and holy in the presence of our God and Father when our Lord Jesus comes with all his holy ones.

1 Thessalonians 3:13

*Weeping may remain for a night,
   but rejoicing comes in the morning.*

Psalm 30:5

*"I will turn their mourning into gladness;
   I will give them comfort and joy instead
      of sorrow," declares the LORD.*

Jeremiah 31:13

Your sun will never set again,
  and your moon will wane no more;
the LORD will be your everlasting light,
  and your days of sorrow will end.

Isaiah 60:20

Why are you downcast, O my soul?
  Why so disturbed within me?
Put your hope in God,
  for I will yet praise him,
  my Savior and my God.

Psalm 42:5–6

Let us hold unswervingly to the hope we profess, for God who promised is faithful.

Hebrews 10:23

I tell you, do not worry about your life, what you will eat or drink; or about your body, what you will wear. Is not life more important than food, and the body more important than clothes? Look at the birds of the air; they do not sow or reap or store away in barns, and yet your heavenly Father feeds them. Are you not much more valuable than they?... Seek first his kingdom and his righteousness, and all these things will be given to you as well.

MATTHEW 6:25–26, 33

Even youths grow tired and weary,
　and young men stumble and fall;
but those who hope in the LORD
　will renew their strength.
They will soar on wings like eagles;
　they will run and not grow weary,
　they will walk and not be faint.

　　　　　　　　　　Isaiah 40:30–31

I waited patiently for the LORD;
　he turned to me and heard my cry.
He lifted me out of the slimy pit,
　out of the mud and mire;
he set my feet on a rock
　and gave me a firm place to stand.
He put a new song in my mouth,
　a hymn of praise to our God.
Many will see and fear
　and put their trust in the LORD.

　　　　　　　　　　Psalm 40:1–3

Promises of Joy *in the* Presence *of* God

God is present in the company of the righteous.

PSALM 14:5

Jesus said, "I will ask the Father, and he will give you another Counselor to be with you forever—the Spirit of truth."

John 14:16–17

You have made known to me the path of life, O LORD;
you will fill me with joy in your presence,
with eternal pleasures at your right hand.

Psalm 16:11

"My Presence will go with you, and I will give you rest," says the LORD.

Exodus 33:14

Do not fear, for I am with you;
*   do not be dismayed, for I am your God.*
I will strengthen you and help you;
*   I will uphold you with my righteous right hand.*

Isaiah 41:10

Let the light of your face shine upon us, O LORD.

Psalm 4:6

Enter his gates with thanksgiving
*   and his courts with praise;*
*   give thanks to him and praise his name.*
For the LORD is good and his love endures forever;
*   his faithfulness continues through all generations.*

Psalm 100:4–5

Where can I go from your Spirit?
Where can I flee from your presence?
If I go up to the heavens, you are there;
if I make my bed in the depths, you are there.
If I rise on the wings of the dawn,
if I settle on the far side of the sea,
even there your hand will guide me,
your right hand will hold me fast.
If I say, "Surely the darkness will hide me
and the light become night around me,"
even the darkness will not be dark to you;
the night will shine like the day,
for darkness is as light to you.
For you created my inmost being;
you knit me together in my mother's womb.
I praise you because I am fearfully and
wonderfully made; your works are
wonderful, I know that full well.

PSALM 139:7–14

The God of love and peace will be with you.

2 Corinthians 13:11

*Blessed are those who have learned to acclaim you,
who walk in the light of your presence, O LORD.*

Psalm 89:15

God has said,
*"Never will I leave you;
never will I forsake you."*
So we say with confidence,
*"The Lord is my helper; I will not be afraid.
What can man do to me?"*

Hebrews 13:5–6

Jesus said, "Peace I leave with you; my peace I give you. I do not give to you as the world gives. Do not let your hearts be troubled and do not be afraid."

John 14:27

"When you pass through the waters,
 I will be with you;
and when you pass through the rivers,
 they will not sweep over you.
When you walk through the fire,
 you will not be burned;
 the flames will not set you ablaze,"
  says the LORD.

Isaiah 43:2

Jesus said,
"I am with you always, to the very end of the age."

MATTHEW 28:20

*The LORD your God is with you,
   he is mighty to save.
He will take great delight in you,
   he will quiet you with his love,
   he will rejoice over you with singing.*

Zephaniah 3:17

Be strong and courageous. Do not be terrified; do not be discouraged, for the LORD your God will be with you wherever you go.

Joshua 1:9

*Blessed are those who dwell
   in your house, LORD;
they are ever praising you.*

Psalm 84:4

I have sought your face with all my heart, O LORD;
be gracious to me according to your promise.

Psalm 119:58

In my integrity you uphold me
and set me in your presence forever.
Praise be to the LORD, the God of Israel,
from everlasting to everlasting.

Psalm 41:12–13

In the presence of the LORD your God, you and your families shall eat and shall rejoice in everything you have put your hand to, because the LORD your God has blessed you.

Deuteronomy 12:7

Blessed are those you choose
   and bring near to live in your courts!
We are filled with the good things
      of your house, LORD,
   of your holy temple.

Psalm 65:4

Send forth your light and your truth,
   let them guide me;
let them bring me to your holy
         mountain,
   to the place where you dwell.
Then will I go to the altar of God,
   to God, my joy and my delight.
I will praise you with the harp,
   O God, my God.

Psalm 43:3–4

Promises of Joy *in the* Blessings *of* God's Love

Your love has given me great joy and encouragement.

PHILEMON 1:7

Jesus said, "Whoever has my commands and obeys them, he is the one who loves me. He who loves me will be loved by my Father, and I too will love him and show myself to him."

John 14:21

I trust in your unfailing love;
 my heart rejoices in your salvation.
I will sing to the LORD,
 for he has been good to me.

Psalm 13:5–6

I will sing of the LORD's great love forever;
 with my mouth I will make your faithfulness
  known through all generations.
I will declare that your love stands firm forever,
 that you established your faithfulness in
  heaven itself.

Psalm 89:1–2

I will be glad and rejoice in your love, LORD,
for you saw my affliction
and knew the anguish of my soul.
You have not handed me over to the enemy
but have set my feet in a spacious place.

Psalm 31:7–8

I am convinced that neither death nor life, neither angels nor demons, neither the present nor the future, nor any powers, neither height nor depth, nor anything else in all creation, will be able to separate us from the love of God that is in Christ Jesus our Lord.

Romans 8:38–39

When I said, "My foot is slipping," your love, O LORD, supported me.

Psalm 94:18

*By day the LORD directs his love,
at night his song is with me—
a prayer to the God of my life.*

Psalm 42:8

*As high as the heavens are above the earth,
so great is his love for those who fear him;
as far as the east is from the west,
so far has he removed our transgressions
from us.
As a father has compassion on his children,
so the LORD has compassion on those who
fear him.*

Psalm 103:11–13

*"As a mother comforts her child,
    so will I comfort you,"
   says the LORD.*

Isaiah 66:13

*Praise the LORD, O my soul;
   all my inmost being, praise his holy
      name.
Praise the LORD, O my soul,
   and forget not all his benefits—
who forgives all your sins
   and heals all your diseases,
who redeems your life from the pit
   and crowns you with love and
      compassion,
who satisfies your desires with good
      things
   so that your youth is renewed like
      the eagle's.*

Psalm 103:1–5

Because of the LORD's great love we
are not consumed,
for his compassions never fail.
They are new every morning;
great is your faithfulness.

Lamentations 3:22–23

The LORD appeared to us
in the past, saying:
"I have loved you with an
everlasting love;
I have drawn you with
loving-kindness."

Jeremiah 31:3

We know that in all things God works for the good of those who love him, who have been called according to his purpose.

Romans 8:28

May your unfailing love rest upon us, O LORD,
even as we put our hope in you.

Psalm 33:22

Though you have not seen Christ, you love him; and even though you do not see him now, you believe in him and are filled with an inexpressible and glorious joy, for you are receiving the goal of your faith, the salvation of your souls.

1 Peter 1:8–9

No eye has seen,
* no ear has heard,*
no mind has conceived
*   what God has prepared for those*
*   who love him.*

1 Corinthians 2:9

Have mercy on me, O God,
  according to your unfailing love;
according to your great compassion
  blot out my transgressions.

Psalm 51:1

From everlasting to everlasting
* the LORD's love is with those who*
*   fear him,*
and his righteousness with their
*   children's children.*

Psalm 103:17

*Show the wonder of your great love,
O God,
you who save by your right hand
those who take refuge in you from
their foes.
Keep me as the apple of your eye;
hide me in the shadow of your wings.*

Psalm 17:7–8

*Your love, O LORD, reaches to the
heavens,
your faithfulness to the skies.
Your righteousness is like the mighty
mountains,
your justice like the great deep.
O LORD, you preserve both man and
beast.
How priceless is your unfailing love!*

Psalm 36:5–7

How great is the love the Father has lavished on us, that we should be called children of God! And that is what we are!

1 JOHN 3:1

No one has ever seen God; but if we love one another, God lives in us and his love is made complete in us.

1 John 4:12

I will betroth you to me forever;
I will betroth you in righteousness
and justice,
in love and compassion.
I will betroth you in faithfulness,
and you will acknowledge the LORD.

Hosea 2:19–20

You are forgiving and good,
O LORD,
abounding in love to all who
call to you.

Psalm 86:5

Because your love is better than life,
*   O LORD,*
*   my lips will glorify you.*
I will praise you as long as I live,
*   and in your name I will lift up*
*   my hands.*
My soul will be satisfied as with the
*   richest of foods;*
*   with singing lips my mouth will*
*   praise you.*
On my bed I remember you;
*   I think of you through the watches*
*   of the night.*
Because you are my help,
*   I sing in the shadow of your wings.*
My soul clings to you;
*   your right hand upholds me.*

Psalm 63:3–8

God so loved the world that he gave his one and only Son, that whoever believes in him shall not perish but have eternal life. For God did not send his Son into the world to condemn the world, but to save the world through him.

JOHN 3:16–17

God demonstrates his own love for us in this: While we were still sinners, Christ died for us.

Romans 5:8

*Let your face shine on your servant;
save me in your unfailing love.*

Psalm 31:16

So we know and rely on the love God has for us. God is love. Whoever lives in love lives in God, and God in him.... There is no fear in love. But perfect love drives out fear.

1 John 4:16, 18

Promises of Joy *in the* Hope *of* Heaven

Rejoice that your names are written in heaven.

LUKE 10:20

Jesus said, "Store up for yourselves treasures in heaven, where moth and rust do not destroy, and where thieves do not break in and steal. For where your treasure is, there your heart will be also."

Matthew 6:20–21

The sun has one kind of splendor, the moon another and the stars another; and star differs from star in splendor. So will it be with the resurrection of the dead. The body that is sown is perishable, it is raised imperishable; it is sown in dishonor, it is raised in glory; it is sown in weakness, it is raised in power; it is sown a natural body, it is raised a spiritual body.

1 Corinthians 15:41–44

The King will say to those on his right, "Come, you who are blessed by my Father; take your inheritance, the kingdom prepared for you since the creation of the world. For I was hungry and you gave me something to eat, I was thirsty and you gave me something to drink, I was a stranger and you invited me in, I needed clothes and you clothed me, I was sick and you looked after me, I was in prison and you came to visit me."

Then the righteous will answer him, "Lord, when did we see you hungry and feed you, or thirsty and give you something to drink? When did we see you a stranger and invite you in, or needing clothes and clothe you? When did we see you sick or in prison and go to visit you?"

The King will reply, "I tell you the truth, whatever you did for one of the least of these brothers of mine, you did for me."

Matthew 25:34–40

The Lord will rescue me from every evil attack and will bring me safely to his heavenly kingdom. To him be glory for ever and ever. Amen.

2 Timothy 4:18

Jesus said, "Whoever acknowledges me before men, I will also acknowledge him before my Father in heaven."

Matthew 10:32

Our citizenship is in heaven. And we eagerly await a Savior from there, the Lord Jesus Christ, who, by the power that enables him to bring everything under his control, will transform our lowly bodies so that they will be like his glorious body.

Philippians 3:20–21

Praise be to the God and Father of our Lord Jesus Christ! In his great mercy he has given us new birth into a living hope through the resurrection of Jesus Christ from the dead, and into an inheritance that can never perish, spoil or fade—kept in heaven for you, who through faith are shielded by God's power until the coming of the salvation that is ready to be revealed in the last time.

1 Peter 1:3–5

Now we know that if the earthly tent we live in is destroyed, we have a building from God, an eternal house in heaven, not built by human hands.

2 Corinthians 5:1

We do not want you to be ignorant about those who fall asleep, or to grieve like the rest of men, who have no hope. We believe that Jesus died and rose again and so we believe that God will bring with Jesus those who have fallen asleep in him. According to the Lord's own word, we tell you that we who are still alive, who are left till the coming of the Lord, will certainly not precede those who have fallen asleep. For the Lord himself will come down from heaven, with a loud command, with the voice of the archangel and with the trumpet call of God, and the dead in Christ will rise first. After that, we who are still alive and are left will be caught up together with them in the clouds to meet the Lord in the air. And so we will be with the Lord forever.

1 THESSALONIANS 4:13–17

At Inspirio we love to hear from you—
your stories, your feedback,
and your product ideas.
Please send your comments to us
by way of e-mail at
icares@zondervan.com
or to the address below:

inspirio™

Attn: Inspirio Cares
5300 Patterson Avenue SE
Grand Rapids, MI 49530

If you would like further information
about Inspirio and the products we
create please visit us at:
www.inspiriogifts.com

Thank you and God Bless!